DISCOVER

THE HEBRIDES

IAIN McGOWAN

HALSGROVE

First published in Great Britain in 2012

Text copyright © Iain McGowan 2012
Image copyright © Iain McGowan 2012

Title page photograph: *Soroby Bay near Balemartine, Tiree.*

British Library Cataloguing-in-Publication Data
A CIP record for this title is available from the British Library

ISBN 978 0 85704 161 6

HALSGROVE
Halsgrove House,
Ryelands Business Park,
Bagley Road, Wellington, Somerset TA21 9PZ
Tel: 01823 653777   Fax: 01823 216796
email: sales@halsgrove.com

Part of the Halsgrove group of companies
Information on all Halsgrove titles is available at: www.halsgrove.com

Printed and bound in China by Everbest Printing Co Ltd

CONTENTS

MAP OF THE HEBRIDES AND SCOTLAND'S WESTERN SEABOARD

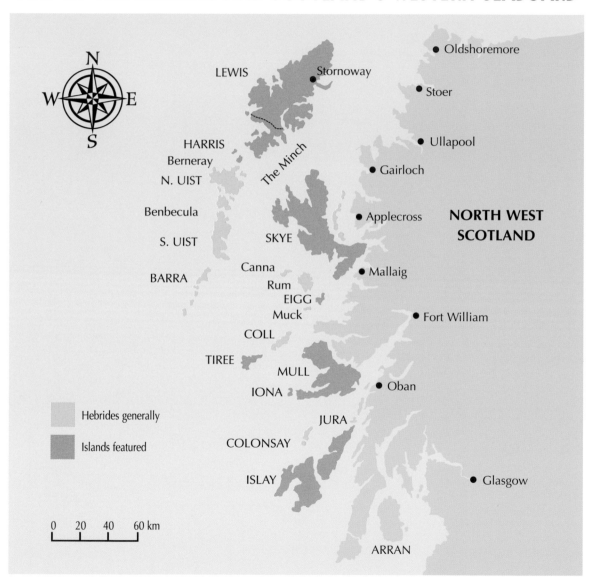

Oldshoremore

Stoer

LEWIS · Stornoway

Ullapool

HARRIS

Berneray · Gairloch

N. UIST

The Minch

Benbecula · Applecross

NORTH WEST SCOTLAND

S. UIST

SKYE

Canna · Mallaig

BARRA

Rum

EIGG

Muck · Fort William

COLL

TIREE

MULL

IONA · Oban

JURA

COLONSAY

ISLAY · Glasgow

☐ Hebrides generally

■ Islands featured

0 20 40 60 km

ARRAN

INTRODUCTION

Land o' Heart's Desire, Isle of Youth,
Dear Western Isle, Gleaming in sunlight …
Margery Kennedy Fraser

Portrait of the Hebrides was published by Halsgrove in 2008 with a re-print in 2011. My intention for the last year or so has been to produce a follow-up volume featuring further images of Scotland's western seaboard and the inclusion of more Hebridean islands. *Portrait of the Hebrides* relied heavily on just the three contrasting islands of Skye, Eigg and Harris with an additional miscellany to give the reader that certain yet almost indefinable spirit and atmosphere so apparent within the Hebrides. This volume includes text and illustrations of Islay, Jura, Mull, Iona, Tiree, Lewis and Berneray with further coverage of Skye, Eigg and Harris to supplement the previous book. For those devotees of the Uists, Barra, Coll, Colonsay, Raasay and the remaining Small Isles, I can only apologise. A challenge for the future perhaps.

A book such as this and the numerous definitive guides published are all based on the simple assumption that the Hebrides are an attraction to the reader who will possibly be eager at some point in time to make the often longish journey to the islands. In the present day of course with all the integrated transport infrastructure available this no longer presents any serious difficulties. However, it was not always so straightforward. The logistics of travel to the 'wild Hebrides' in the eighteenth century for example would for many have proved to be an almost insurmountable challenge. There was an enormous degree of uncertainty and a real fear of the unknown to be overcome first. Fortunately Johnson and Boswell achieved the journey in the 1780s, Walter Scott visited in 1814, Mendelssohn on his famous voyage discovered Fingal's Cave in 1829 whilst Robert Buchanan arrived in 1873. By then the islands had been put on 'The Tour' and the rest is history.

Except that opinions differed amongst these early explorers. We know of Boswell's enthusiasm and reception that he and Johnson received – "the hospitality of this remote region is like that of the golden age". We know too of Robert Buchanan's questioning whether "the British lover of beauty … finds anywhere a picture more exquisite than opens out, vista after vista, among these wondrous isles". Mendelssohn's *Hebrides* Overture could only have been written by someone singularly at one with the sights, sounds and rhythm of Staffa. But it was John Spencer-Stanhope in 1806 who perhaps sounded a more cautious note – "Talk not to me of bad roads! What can you know of travelling who have not gone starving, frozen, sleepless and supperless, in real danger of death by bog, torrent or exposure. Such is the journey to the Hebrides and none but the hardy need undertake it". Walter Scott's perception of the Skye Cuillin and Loch Coruisk in 1814 was equally unenthusiastic – "Rarely human eye has known a scene so stern as that dread lake, with its dark ledge of barren stone".

Herein perhaps lies one of the fascinations of the Hebrides and Western Scotland – this variation of thought, impression and idea. At a time when naturalists were beginning to set foot in variously unknown parts of the globe, the west coast of Scotland could have been located on a different planet! Many European capitals were nearer to London and it was clear in which direction most journeys were undertaken.

Thank goodness then for today's enlightenment, our appreciation of the island's varying moods, their colour, their history and peace. For many the ever changing weather, space and isolation is now an attraction. Whether hidden by curtains of Atlantic rain, boldly silhouetted in evening light or faint and mysterious through a blanket of mist there is always an allure, an enticement for the visitor to return. This book – a further portrait – is also intended as a temptation, to at least interest the reader in considering journeying to these islands before too many changes occur. Before that timeless quality that John MacCulloch found and famously wrote of in the early nineteenth century is eventually eroded and before the elements of continuity of a unique lifestyle are finally broken.

The dramatic scenery of Glen Sannox on Arran looking towards Cir Mhor (798m). Often known as 'Scotland in Miniature', Arran has an incredibly diverse variety of landscapes ranging from high craggy peaks, wild lonely glens, extensive open moorland, considerable areas of forest and numerous bays, beaches and inlets. As such it has in places both the character of the Scottish Highlands and the Hebrides and is therefore a fitting location for the start of this western seaboard and island photographic journey.

THE WESTERN SEABOARD
Arran to Applecross

Sandstone detail, Corrie, Arran

In describing and illustrating a series of different islands, each with their own distinctive personality, it seems meaningful and prudent to place text and photographs in the context of the islands' surroundings. In the case of the Hebrides this involves the featuring of parts of the Scottish western seaboard and its associated hinterland. It is this thinking that has promoted the first two chapters of this book covering what many observers would consider as the most dramatic and scenically exciting coastline in Britain. Between the island of Arran in the south - never strictly regarded as a Hebridean island – and the lonely, bare shores around Sutherland at the top of Scotland, the power of wind, fire, ice and sea have created over countless millions of years an area of breathtaking geological beauty. High mountains, deep fjord-like lochs, sweeping bays, contorted rocks and stacks and in more recent times a unique social history have all combined to form the very foundation of the Hebridean islands' particular location as being at the western extremity of European civilisation. In this first chapter the book travels north from Arran, skirting the Argyll coast and finally reaching the wilder emptiness of the Torridon region and its Applecross peninsula.

Looking across the 200m wide Argyll Cuan Sound from Seil to the island of Luing. Seil together with Luing and Easdale are often referred to as the Slate Islands, quarrying of slate at one time being their predominant industry with most of the villages constructed originally to house quarry families. Cullipool, the principal village on Luing once employed some 150 workers in its quarries producing over 700,000 slates each year until final closure in 1965.

Coastal slate outcrop with the old village and quay of Easdale, formerly known as Ellanbeich, beyond. In the nineteenth century it was an important stop for ships collecting the slate. Here the quarries reached down to a depth of 75m until they were breached by the sea after a violent storm in November 1881.

Cullipool with evidence of its industrial past. *Top left:* The slate-covered beach overlooking the sound of Luing. *Top right:* Slate harbour walling. *Above left:* Abandoned slate quarry face. *Above right:* White painted quarry workers' cottages, many of which are now holiday homes.

Near the centre of Luing above the fertile fields of Toberonochy stands the isolated ruin of Kilchatton Chapel abandoned in the seventeenth century. The numerous slate headstones surrounding the chapel are testament to the many quarry workers buried here and to the dangers and hardship that existed in the industry not just on Luing but also on the more remote outlying islands of Fladda and Balnahua.

Scattered remains of the slate industry on the minute island of Easdale. The outline of some of the drowned quarries can still be seen together with the island of Mull in the far distance.

Opposite: Early morning mood looking out from Oban harbour down to the sound of Mull with Mull itself on the left in the far distance and the sunlit northern tip of Kerrera in the foreground. Following the arrival of the railway in the latter half of the nineteenth century, Oban grew rapidly to become the principal port in the south-west highlands and still used today by fishermen and numerous summer visitors. With its considerable network of ferries linking many of the islands, the port is often referred to as 'the gateway to the Hebrides'.

Late afternoon reflections, Castle Stalker, Appin. Constructed on a small rocky outcrop known as Cormorant Rock, the isolated castle on the shores of Loch Linnhe was once a stronghold of the Stewarts of Appin. Originally built by the MacDougalls in the thirteenth century it has been surmised that the forfeiture of the Lordship of the Isles in the fifteenth century was ordered from here by James IV. Since then the building has been almost totally rebuilt and in recent times extensively restored.

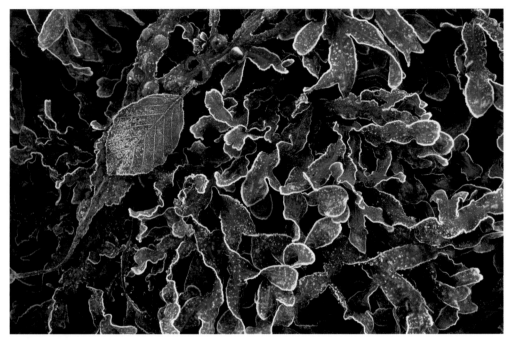

Frost encrusted seaweed, Loch Leven.

The shapely snow-covered 1022m peak of Buachaille Etive Mor, seen here from the frozen river Etive, heralds the eastern approach to Glencoe from Rannoch Moor. Glencoe known as the 'Glen of Weeping' due to its infamous massacre of the MacDonalds in 1692 is still one of Scotland's wildest glens resembling an enormous trough within magnificent and often moody mountain scenery where the frequent cloud, mist or rain can add to the pathos of its history. To the south, Argyll's highest peak, the 1150m Bidean nam Bian, and to the north the narrow precipitous Aonach Eagach ridge act, as constant Meccas for both walkers and climbers enjoying this outstanding area.

First light at dawn hits the distant 1126m Ben Cruachan and nearby hills flanking Glen Etive.

The view west across Rannoch Moor towards the sunlit peaks of Meall Odhar, Clach Leathad and Stob Ghabhar. Crossing the desolate moor, via the A82 trunk road, often shrouded in driving rain can sometimes be an utterly depressing experience. Yet on occasions, particularly in winter and with a fresh fall of snow, there is a certain, almost magical appeal about the landscape as shown here.

Looking towards the same mountains across Lochan na h-Aclaise.

A freshly exposed stand of coniferous forest near Achriabhach, Glen Nevis.

Opposite: Stormy conditions over the lower flanks of Ben Nevis and Aonach Beag seen from the upper reaches of Glen Nevis. For many Glen Nevis is regarded as the finest glen in Scotland with a variety of scenery and panoramas almost unsurpassed. In the lower glen, leading from Fort William, the soft green fields and stands of silver birch line the winding river gradually giving way to the harsher, wilder upper glen with its rushing waterfalls, rock faces and dramatic mountain views. On one side the highest mountain group in Britain stretches eastwards in a series of peaks to Loch Treig whilst on the other the Mamore range separates the glen from neighbouring Loch Leven. At Steall, one of the three highest waterfalls in Scotland drops down an outlying cliff of Sgurr a' Mhaim for almost 120m whilst below Ben Nevis the 400m long waterslide of Allt Coire Eoghainn, especially after rain, provides an unforgettable sight.

The view looking north-east from a shoulder of Sgurr Finnisg-aig above the Leanachan Forest and River Lochy.

A mural at Mallaig celebrates the port's fishing history. At one time the town was the most important herring and shellfish port on the west coast and of Britain, the value of its catches far exceeding that of Oban. With the slow decline of the fishing industry in recent years, Mallaig's activities have increasingly been given over to ferry services particularly to the Small Isles group and neighbouring island of Skye with occasional sailings to the Western Isles. Cruises and excursions are also available to nearby Knoydart.

Frosted trees below Loch Cluanie make a spectacular, almost monochromatic scene in the early light of a bitterly cold winter's morning.

Travelling north from Loch Alsh and Loch Carron, the West Highlands start to take on a bleaker character. The landscape becomes more exposed to strong winds, less fertile and with far fewer trees. The population is more scattered, the roads emptier. Initially there are fewer routes to the coast with the exception of the dramatic road over the Bealach na Ba' pass to Applecross and beyond around the peninsula of the same name to Sheildaig. Even today with its numerous sharp bends and steep gradients the pass can still be a considerable challenge for many motorists. The photograph shows typical mountain scenery at the base of the pass with Sgurr a' Chaorachain (776m) on the left.

Along the undulating coast road from Applecross, the views open up westwards to the islands of Raasay and Skye. The tiny hamlets such as Lonbain, Callakille, Cuaig and Fearnmore struggle for a lonely existence against the harsher elements of weather here. This view near Lonbain gives a striking impression of the nature of this utterly empty land with its crumbling buildings and abandoned crofts.

Late afternoon sunshine and shadows on the snow-capped flanks of Liathach (1024m) viewed from across Upper Loch Torridon near Sheildaig. With Beinn Alligin and Beinn Eighe, these mountains form the dramatic heart of the spectacular Torridon region so beloved of walkers, climbers and geologists. From here onwards our journey north beyond Loch Maree and Gairloch takes us to even wilder locations.

Mellon Udrigle. The coastal district north of Gairloch contains numerous small scattered communities spread along a variety of narrow roads centered around Loch Ewe, Loch Gairloch and Gruinard Bay. Names such as Red Point, Opinan, Port Henderson, Melvaig, Naast, Mellanguan, Cove, Aultbea and Mellon Charles immediately bring to mind scenes of this often wild, inhospitable, yet sometimes beautiful area. Turning north from Laide brings one to a second township with the name of Opinan and nearby the broad sands of Mellon Udrigle. Looking east across Gruinard Bay to the far distant peaks of Sutherland, the sands are backed by short turf, low sandstone hills and a few isolated cottages. On a fine sunny day the sea views are some of the finest in northwest Scotland.

THE WESTERN SEABOARD
Opinan to Oldshoremore

Abandoned church interior, Cove.

The two chapters in this book on the western seaboard are as a result of the number of photographs intended for inclusion and as a simple divide between the relatively fertile, richer areas south of Gairloch and the dramatic, bleaker, harder countryside to the north. One chapter would have been too long. In this second chapter the book continues generally following a coastal route from the Loch Ewe/Gruinard Bay area of Wester Ross north to Ullapool, into Sutherland and onwards through Coigach and Assynt up to the Reay Forest terminating at Oldshoremore.

DANGEROUS
BUILDING
KEEP OUT

Wartime structures, Cove. During the Second World War Loch Ewe was used both as a Naval Fleet base and as the starting point for many of the Arctic Convoys sailing to Murmansk in Russia. Even today the Loch still acts as a reserve anchorage. On its western shore a long winding road finally leads to Cove beyond which can be found a simple stone memorial to all those who died in appalling conditions during the convoy operations. Scattered around this bleak, exposed site are what have been described as one of the finest remaining collections of concrete WWII defensive and observational structures left in the country, some of which are occasionally open to the public. This view looks south down the loch to the distant Torridon hills.

From Laide skirting the back edge of Gruinard Bay, the coast is lined with further old crofting townships with names such as Sand, First Coast, Second Coast and others long forgotten or abandoned in some of the small woodlands now growing along the shore. The photograph here from First Coast shows the often rugged nature of this coastline with its spurs, crags and hills of grey gneiss rock.

Destitution Road. Continuing along what is now the main A832 coastal route after Gruinard Bay and passing Dundonnell and the wooded Strath Beag, the road rises to the desolate moors of Dundonnell Forest at over 300m. Here it is known throughout the north west Highlands as Destitution Road for it was constructed during the times of famine in the 1850s to give work for starving people. Short, scattered, broken lengths of protective snow fencing still line the road as shown here. The sunlit slopes of Beinn Dearg (1084m) are in the background.

Looking back along the road towards Dundonnell, the empty cottage adding a suitable pathos to this bleak location.

Stac Pollaidh and Cul Mor from Aird of Coigach. North of Ullapool and into Sutherland and its Coigach district the scenery changes utterly to give way to a desert of moorland and rock broken only by numerous small rivers and lochans and the sometimes strange upstanding silhouettes of isolated mountains rearing up from their surrounds. Here the Inverpolly National Nature Reserve was declared in 1961 and covers an area of some 27,000 acres taking in the peaks of Stac Pollaidh, Cul Mor and Cul Beag to form one of the last great wilderness areas left in Britain.

Early morning mist and low cloud over Stac Pollaidh. Despite being only 613m high, the distinctive outline of Stac Pollaidh gives the impression of the mountain being much higher. As such it has become one of the most recognised profiles in Scotland with its splintered and spired summit and a popular location for walkers and climbers.

The view from the summit of Stac Pollaidh showing the true nature of much of the Sutherland landscape and the distant peaks of Suilven, Cul Mor, Canisp and Quinag.

Winter reflections of snow-capped Cul Mor (849m) from across Lochan an Ais.

Above: The view south across Badentarbat Bay to the Summer Isles from near Altandhu. The village of Achiltibuie on the western shore of the Coigach peninsula is on the left just out of the picture. Achiltibuie was once an active fishing centre but now most of the fishing is for sport. From here however boat trips are available to take visitors to the deserted Summer Isles of which the largest, Tanera Mor, once had a population of over 70 as late as 1900.

Right: School bus stop, Acheninver, Achiltibuie.

Opposite: A wide-angle scene from Achnahaird on the Coigach peninsula across typically boggy Sutherland moorland to the distant mountains, Stac Pollaidh being particularly visible on the right.

Frost covered trees and winter reflections in Cam Loch by Elphin

Low mist and cloud sweep over the summit of Beinn Uidhe (740m) viewed from near Skiag Bridge, Assynt.

Ardvreck Castle, Assynt. Built in 1597 as the seat of MacLeod of Assynt, only the ruined tower of the castle now remains on its grassy point overlooking Loch Assynt. Following a siege in 1672, the castle was taken by the MacKenzies who built the nearby Calda House around 1726. Later destroyed by fire, this too is now a picturesque ruin.

Beyond Loch Assynt and looking west from near Unapool to the seven peaks of Quinag (808m), one of the most distinctive mountains in the area.

Opposite: Morning mood, Loch Assynt. The 11km loch is notably divided into two halves by character, the western end with its shores and tiny islands bearing woodland and old pines whilst the eastern end is utterly bare and featureless apart from Ardvreck Castle.

Late afternoon winter light on the road from the Rhu Stoer peninsula to Kylesku photographed near Drumbeg with the outline of Quinag in the background. The road is a long one leading from the more fertile straths of the peninsula and keeping mostly inland to avoid the deeply riven coastline. Riding switchback over the rock and winding between lochans and crags, it passes numerous tiny communities such as Clachtoll, Stoer, Drumbeg and Nedd and isolated homes of a distinctly alpine character.

Clashnessie Bay. The broad reddish sands of Clashnessie Bay at the base of the Rhu Stoer peninsula look out towards Oldany Island and the distant Eddrachillis Bay still a favourite area for lobster fishermen. For those driving along the road referred to opposite, Clashnessie makes an excellent break and an opportunity to explore this fascinating coast-line in more detail.

Left: The ruined and roofless church at Stoer on its hill overlooking the village and the sea.

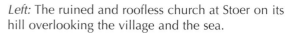

Reflections in a hut window at Fanagmore.

Left: A typical roadside croft cottage near Rienachait.

North of Assynt, the Reay Forest stretches almost to the top of Scotland. The mountains at its western fringe lie further inland and between these and the coast the low ground is some of the roughest and poorest in the Highlands. Sparsely populated only along its shores there is no habitation inland. This photograph taken near Foindle looking over Loch Laxford gives a good impression of this bleak, unforgiving landscape.

Late afternoon on the minor road following Loch Inchard from Rhiconich to Achlyness and Rhimichie.

Opposite: Cloud and reflection at Oldshoremore. From the small fishing port of Kinlochbervie on the north side of Loch Inchard, the road continues to the crofts of Oldshoremore, Oldshore Beg, Blairmore, Droman and Sheigra. At Oldshoremore the sandy beach is one of the finest in Sutherland and reputed to be the anchorage of King Haakon's fleet in August 1263 at the start of his invasion of Scotland. Beyond the road end at Sheigra a rough track leads to Sandwood Bay, the coast then continuing north to its final turning point at Cape Wrath. From here then, there is no alternative but to go west – towards the Hebrides.

The Rinns of Islay. Islay is almost an island of two halves, not just in spirit but physically with its two masses nearly separated by the sea lochs of Loch Indaal and Loch Gruinart leaving a narrow isthmus some 2 miles wide between. Both masses are utterly unalike in appearance, the flat moorlands, fields and low undulating hills of the western half known as the Rinns being almost devoid of trees and windswept from the Atlantic, whilst the more mountainous eastern half with its degree of sheltered valleys and coast provides the richer farmland that supports many of the island's population. Despite exposure to the prevailing winds, the multi-coloured patchwork of the Rinns provides superb grazing for cattle and in the more sheltered hollows arable crops are still grown. This view of the Rinns moorland not far from Kilchoman gives an impression of the wide open spaces of this area.

ISLAY AND JURA
Wind, Wildlife and Whisky

Tractor and bracken, the Rinns.

The southern Hebridean islands are thought to be the first Scottish islands colonised by man with Islay later becoming the seat of government of the Lord of the Isles with its administrative headquarters at Loch Finlaggan. As a form of 'capital' of the Hebrides this principality by the fourteenth and fifteenth centuries was strong enough to make its own terms with neighbouring countries but over succeeding centuries through strife, battle and greed this importance finally lapsed. Today the islands of Islay and Jura are often linked by association; they are physically very close separated only by the narrow Sound of Islay but remarkably different in character. Islay has its farms and fertility, Jura is predominantly a rugged, hilly wilderness. Islay is famous for its whisky, outstanding wildlife and archaeology whilst Jura although also producing whisky has little botanical variety, many deer, a much smaller population and few historical remains. A regular ferry crosses the sound between Port Askaig on Islay to Feolin on Jura.

Doorway at Bowmore. Bowmore, the centre of Islay is one of the few Scottish 'planned villages' to be built in the Hebrides. Many were constructed on the mainland arising out of a series of agricultural estate reoganisations in the eighteenth and nineteenth centuries and in the case of Islay particularly due to its fertility. As such Bowmore is notable for its wide principal street and layout.

The interior of Bowmore's eighteenth century parish church of Kilarrow built to a circular plan at the head of the principal street. It has been said that the church was constructed in this manner without corners so that the Devil would have no place to hide therein.

Evening light on the ruins of Kilnave Chapel on the west shore of Loch Gruinart with its cross dating back to about AD 750. The loch is well known as a refuge for the over-wintering Barnacle and Greenland white-fronted geese that appear in great numbers between late September and early October. Between 20,000 to 30,000 birds have been recorded here.

Kildalton Cross. The Kildalton ringed High Cross at the Kildalton Chapel near Ardmore Point is thought to have been carved by a sculptor from Iona around AD800. Almost 3m high from a single piece of blue stone and with its numerous symbols and motifs, it is now regarded as one of the finest Celtic relics in Scotland. The many carvings, chapels, crannogs, standing stones, duns, forts and chambered cairns to be found on Islay all tell of the island's rich pre-history.

The Paps of Jura. The extensive wilderness of heather, bracken and rock that forms most of Jura culminates in its most prominent feature – the three Paps. These three conical mountains grouped around Loch an t-Siob and all over 700m high not only dominate the island but in clear weather with their distinctive profiles can be seen from great distances around. This view of Beinn Shiantaidh (757m), the Holy Mountain, clearly shows the vast scree slopes of quartzite that are also such a notable feature.

Sunshine and Jura House gardens. By contrast with the general island surroundings, the Jura House gardens are a delightful oasis of colour, softness and light with the house itself encircled by further woodlands and rhododendrons overlooking the Sound of Islay and Brosdale Island. To arrive here in summer after a hard day's walking and sample the contents of the 'tea tent' is simply pure heaven!

Whisky. Islay and Jura are renowned for their malt whisky. Islay in particular is often known as the whisky island and a considerable workforce is employed by its eight distilleries. Bowmore dates from 1779 with Lagavulin even earlier. In addition there are Ardbeg, Bunnahabhain, Bruichladdich, Caol Ila, Laphroaig and Port Ellen. About four million gallons of whisky are produced from these distilleries each year, much of which is exported. On Jura the recently constructed distillery at Craighouse bottled its first malt in 1974, the building replacing the old nineteenth century structure. The photographs show whisky barrels at Caol Ila and Craighouse awaiting further use.

Opposite: High summer on the Rinns of Islay near Kilchiaran.

Peat cutting on Islay is still carried out extensively both on the Rinns and also along the flanks of Laggan Bay. Some of the peat is for domestic use but much of it is required by the whisky industry. At times the degree of cutting has caused strong disagreements with the views of the nature conservationists but the more recent designation of certain areas as National Nature Reserves has helped ease some of these difficulties. The photograph shows cut peat on the Rinns laid out to dry with the eastern hills in the far distance.

A soft misty day on the old road between Bridgend and Port Ellen near Glen Machrie. The telegraph poles seem to be a particular feature of the scene. A new road was later built to the west via Bowmore and now serving Islay's airport. Bridgend was the home village of the former laird's mansion Islay House whilst Port Ellen is the largest centre of population, its harbour first constructed in the 1820s, accommodating many of the mainland ferries.

The two white-painted villages of (top) Port Charlotte and (bottom) Portnahaven. With its title of Queen of the Rinns, Port Charlotte was built in the early eighteenth century by a local minister, Rev. MacLaurin, each house being identical in plan and size, and is now a popular holiday destination. Portnahaven near Rinns Point at the southern extremity of the Rinns was once a fishing village separated only by a small burn from its twin village Port Wemyss. From here Northern Ireland's Antrim coast is only some 55km away.

Morning calm across Loch Indaal viewed from near Bruichladdich looking almost south to Laggan Point and the far distant Mull of Oa.

A quiet afternoon, Kintra, Mull. Situated at the very tip of the long projecting Ross of Mull, Kintra looks northwest towards Iona, Staffa and the Treshnish Isles with the distant Small Isles often visible on a clear, calm day such as this. At nearby Bull Hole a derelict stone jetty acts as a reminder of the period when the beautiful pink granite of this part of Mull was quarried here and used in the construction of such prestigious projects as Holborn Viaduct, Blackfriars Bridge and the Albert Memorial in London.

MULL AND IONA
Hills, Headlands and History

Coastal colour, Fidden, Ross of Mull.

The third largest island of the Hebrides and statistically the wettest, Mull lies west of Oban separated from the mainland by the long Sound of Mull. Due to its convoluted profile its coastline is at least 500km, etched in the west by a series of deep sea lochs. Mainly volcanic of basalt and schist, with the primary exception of the pink granite butt of the Ross of Mull, the interior is extremely bare, rugged and hilly rising at its highest to the shapely 966m Ben More. Most of Mull's inhabitants live on or very near the coast partly governed by the island's geology and partly by its network of single carriageway roads. Surrounded by a series of interesting islands – Ulva, Gometra, Staffa, the Treshnish Isles, Eorsa and Inch Kenneth to name but a few – Iona is by far the best known mainly due to its religious foundation as the cradle of Scottish Christianity and learning. Visitors come here throughout the year from all parts of the world to enjoy Iona's sacred and monastic buildings, its purity of colour and an overriding sense of peace and mysticism.

The road to Iona. A milepost and the view to Ben More from near Pennyghael along what is now the main A849 road between Salen and Fionnphort looking across Loch Scridain. The road, now heavily used by coaches and traffic carrying visitors from the Caledonian MacBrayne ferry at Craignure through Glen More and down via the Ross of Mull to the Iona ferry at Fionnphort, was considerably improved in the late nineteenth century with these sometimes painted mileposts acting as a distinctive feature. Ben More, often covered in cloud, is a remnant of the Mull volcano active some 50-60 million years ago. Much of the island's less mountainous land whilst generally basalt based is nevertheless barren after the large degree of sheep farming introduced in the nineteenth century following the infamous Highland Clearances.

Carsaig House. A minor road from Pennyghael leads down to the dramatic coastline at Carsaig with its south facing bay, headlands and well known walk under the cliffs to the Nun's Cave and Carsaig Arches rock formations. The beautiful nineteenth-century house on the hillside leading up to Beinn Charsaig looks out over some of the most fertile ground on Mull to the distant islands of Colonsay, Islay and Jura.

The view south from near Killiemor looking over Loch na Keal to the empty central mountain mass around Ben More. It is Loch na Keal in particular that gives Mull its distinctive outline with the Loch almost cutting the island into two parts, only the narrow isthmus leading to Salen remaining. Along the southern coast of the outer loch, opposite the island of Inch Kenneth, the slopes of Ben More rounding Craig Mhór fall in dramatic 250m cliffs near Gribun with their associated rockfalls and gigantic isolated boulders.

Storm clouds over Mull's south eastern coast and hills viewed from across the Firth of Lorn.

Lip na Cloiche. In contrast to Mull's generally wild, barren landscape, the house and gardens of Lip na Cloiche near the western coast overlooking Loch Tuath and the island of Ulva provide an oasis of calm, colour and fertility. The densely planted garden , with its imaginative use of 'found' objects integrating the garden with the landscape, provides numerous home propagated plants for sale being open for visitors throughout the year.

A beautiful summer's evening across freshly cut fields near Gruline at the head of Loch na Keal with Ben More beyond. A mausoleum is sited here dedicated to major General Lachlan Macquarrie of Ulva, the first Governor of New South Wales and 'father of Australia'.

The waterfront, Tobermory. Capital of Mull and one of the most attractive small towns in Scotland, Tobermory was laid out and built by the British Fisheries Society in the late eighteenth century. With its numerous brightly painted houses forming a colourful backdrop to its busy harbour, the town is featured in countless magazines, travel guides, books and calendars every year. Sunken in the bay is the *San Juan de Sicilia* wrecked in its attempt to escape from the ill-fated Spanish Armada of 1588 and from which numerous efforts have been made to extract the treasure thought to be still on board.

The ruins of Crackaig. The story of the Highland Clearances is one that was repeated all over Western Scotland and the Hebrides when tenants were ruthlessly evicted and cleared from their homes and land during the nineteenth century in favour of sheep farming. Now regarded as one of the most shameful episodes of British history, the effect of these clearances is still apparent throughout the Highlands and Islands where signs of earlier habitation can easily be found. On Mull the population fell from around 10,600 in the 1820s to below 4000 by the end of the same century, many forcibly emigrated to the new worlds of America, Canada or Australia. Crackaig on the hilly moorland peninsula north of Burg and overlooking the Treshnish Islands was once an extensive village of some 200 souls – all removed. *Right:* The outline of a sailing vessel can still be seen carved on one of the remaining stones of a ruined cottage doorway. It depicts a boat typical of the mid nineteenth century.

This page and opposite: Aspects of Iona. Reached by frequent ferry across the narrow sound of Iona from Fionnphort, the diminutive island of Iona some 2 x 5 km has a religious history thought to extend back to the distant Iron Age long before Columba who arrived here in 563. It was Columba however who in the course of some thirty years established the first monastery and turned Iona into a centre of pilgrimage and Christian learning famed throughout Europe. The island's subsequent history of numerous Norse raids over five centuries and consequent rebuilding ultimately laid the foundations of the historic buildings still to be seen today with the outstanding abbey, dating from 1500 now given cathedral status, being finally restored by the Church of Scotland in the early 1900s. *Above:* The glorious pale sands of the north beach (the White Strand of the Monks) on a 'soft' day overlooking the nearby tip of the Ross of Mull and the more distant Ardmeanach headland.

Fingals Cave, Staffa. In 1829 the composer Felix Mendelssohn visited Fingals Cave on the tiny volcanic island of Staffa and was subsequently inspired to write his overture *The Hebrides.* As a result of his visit and an earlier one by Sir Joseph Banks, President of the Royal Society in 1772 and consequent publicity, Staffa has become one of the best known islands in Europe receiving numerous visitors each year, weather and tides permitting. Set in a colonnade of black hexagonal columns known as the Great Face, the 75m-deep cave is just one of a series of caves to be found on Staffa with Clamshell, Boat and Cormorant being almost as impressive. Similar columnar basaltic lava pavements and features can also be found at the Giant's Causeway in Ireland's County Antrim.

Deserted village, Lunga. The isolated and uninhabited Treshnish Isles lie some 16 km beyond the north western coast of Mull. Consisting of four principal islands Fladda, Lunga, Bac Mor or Dutchman's Cap and Bac Beag, they are part of the same basaltic structure as Staffa and Mull. Home to numerous seabirds and particularly Puffins on Lunga, the islands can be visited from Mull or Iona but only on fine, calm, summer days. Lunga, the largest of the islands, once had a population of about 20 but since 1857 has been uninhabited. The photograph shows a part of the deserted village overlooking a stoney spit known as Corran Lunga with the more distant Fladda, Gometra and northern Mull beyond.

Balevulin Bay, Tiree. Sun, sea and sand – the very essence of Tiree. Balevulin Bay with its dazzling beauty of pure white shell sand is typical of many of Tiree's beaches. Behind these beaches, the rich flower-scented machair extends back to fields of clover, buttercup, pansy, silverweed and wild thyme – home to numerous hares (there are no rabbits) and the song of countless skylarks.

TIREE
Sun, Sea and Sand

Hand-written sign near Barrapol.

Tiree and neighbouring Coll are the most westerly of the Inner Hebrides, Tiree being some 30km out beyond Mull's Treshnish Point. Often described as the land beneath the waves, this almost flat, fertile island lifting to only a few metres above wave level is still home to a comparatively large, thriving, crofting community., There are just two hills, Ben Hynish (141m) and Ben Hough (119m). On average the climate on Tiree from May to September is the sunniest in Britain but also the windiest. Once known as the Granary of the Isles, it is this wind and the subsequent wind-blown shell sand covering much of the island that has created the richness of soil and machair. It is also the wind that has helped make Tiree an almost 'midge-free' environment during the summer months!

Walker's bothy near Vaul. Many visitors to Tiree simply walk. The flat landscape with few cars on the narrow roads and the island's general ambience, particularly during the summer months, are a great encouragement to don the walking boots and haversack and to discover the great outdoors. It is also reckoned that one can distinguish a Tiree man by his leaning gait, a result of years of walking into the almost constant prevailing wind.

Spotty house with washing, Sandaig. Tiree has been described as a living museum of croft houses, growing out of the unique flatness of its land. There are thatched houses, black felters, spotty houses, pudding and plain. Spotty houses are those built of stone, dormer windowed and with only the mortar painted, the stones themselves remaining uncovered.

A golden landscape. Fields of buttercup looking across to Kirkapol and distant Scarinish from near Vaul. Where there is restricted access for sheep, the flowers thrive in a spectacular order of colour - from the mauve of wild orchids in May and June, through a yellow haze of buttercup and daisy, the reds and pinks of clover and ragged robin to the purple of knapweed in August. Here the rich flora of the machair is seen in its early yellow phase.

The Ringing Stone near Balephetrish is a large erratic boulder carried to Tiree by glacial action. Covered by prehistoric cup markings, the stone 'rings' loudly when struck by a small rock.

Dun Mor Vaul close to Vaul Bay dates back as a stone broch to about the first century BC replacing an earlier timber structure on the same site. Possibly built as a communal refuge, the circular double stone walls 4m thick contained a series of galleries linked by staircases providing shelter when necessary.

Traditional thatched cottage near Middleton now used as part of a heritage museum. Once a 'black house' with walling almost 3m thick and a central hearth in the floor, the building has been modernised to a 'white house' with the addition of a more conventional fireplace and chimney, cemented walls and whitewash. The thatching is still contained within the outer walling for wind protection.

A dramatic contrast to the more conventional architecture of Tiree, the new ferry passenger shelter close to Scarinish Pier has attracted much comment and discussion. An open corridor between two thick concrete walls gives protection against the often extreme winds at this exposed site whilst also leading to an enclosed part-glazed cabin for use in wet conditions.

Soroby Bay near Balemartine looking towards Crossapol. The intense colours of the sea are typical of those found around many of the Hebridean Islands where water lies over sandy beaches or under clear blue summer skies.

Marram grass behind the coast at Ruaig above Gott Bay with a typical scattering of white-painted Tiree housing. Many of the island's communities tend to be in a ragged, spread-out form rather than a more conventional closely spaced village.

Granite light-keepers' cottages, Hynish. The most south westerly point of Tiree, Hynish was chosen by Alan Stevenson in 1838 as the centre for the construction of the 42m high Skerryvore lighthouse and later as the shore station for the lighthouse-keepers and their families. The lighthouse built with granite shipped from Mull is situated on the Skerryvore reef about 20km from Hynish and was completed in 1843. The Hebridean Trust's Hynish Heritage Trail takes visitors around the old harbour, dry dock, pier and various ancillary buildings to the cottages and adjacent signal tower once used to convey messages to the lighthouse.

Opposite: The colours of a cloudy morning on Balephetrish Bay.

The Skye Cuillins. The view looking almost south from Sligachan through the Red Hills towards the isolated Bla Bheinn range. For many Skye is the most scenically spectacular and diverse of all the Hebridean islands arising particularly from its centrepiece of the Red Hills and dramatic Black Cuillin. There is a certain degree of softness with the smooth profiled, rounded, granite Red Hills rising to the 776m summit of Glamaig – there is none with the craggy, spiky, jagged coarse-grained gabbro of the Black Cuillin whose 13km sawtooth horseshoe traverse offers the most exciting day's mountaineering in the country. The Black Cuillin contains no fewer than 22 Munros (peaks over 3000') culminating in Sgurr Alasdair (992m) and of all these summits very few can be reached without advanced rock climbing skills. The two peaks of Bla Bheinn (928m) and Garbh-bheinn (806m) although isolated from the Black Cuillin by Glen Sligachan are still considered by many to be part of the main range.

SKYE AND LEWIS
Mountain, Moorland and Mood

Empty cottage window, Carbost, Skye.

Despite being separated by The Minch, the two largest islands in the Hebrides, Skye in the Inner Hebrides and Lewis in the Western Isles or Outer Hebrides have in certain respects much in common. Both have extensive wild, infertile, empty moorland and both also have ranges of high hills. There is a large active community in both islands with integrated public transport and ferries and also many of the services and conveniences taken for granted in the twenty-first century. However in the manner of all islands, there are certain individual characteristics. On Skye there is only one attractive, typically Hebridean beach – there are many on Lewis. Skye has the Black Cuillin mountain range, utterly unique, there is nothing else like it in Britain. Patches of deciduous woodland can be found in Skye especially around Sleat whilst on Lewis trees struggle for survival. For some Skye has a certain romantic appeal arising from its history and musical heritage – the misty isle terminology does not fit with Lewis. But perhaps above all Skye is considered in certain minds not even to be an island since linked by its relatively new bridge to the mainland. Lewis with adjoining Harris certainly is.

Passing place, the road to Glen Eynort. The high moorland either side of the main A863 road from Sligachan to Dunvegan is particularly windswept and bare and especially on the Minginish peninsula from Drynoch westwards to both Talisker and Glen Eynort. Here the hills 300 - 400m high seem to bear down on the narrow roads and always in the background the serrated outline of the Black Cuillin is present. This view looking north from the Glen Eynort road above Carbost gives an indication of this lonely area. Beyond the tiny hamlet of Eynort and under the shadow of Beinn Buidhe na Creige can be found the abandoned crofting township of Tuasdale cleared in the 1840s, another example of mid nineteenth century agricultural 'improvement'.

Opposite: Morning calm across Broadford Bay looking towards Pabbay and the distant Applecross peninsula and Torridon Hills.

Late afternoon light at Sligachan looking south down Glen Sligachan to Marsco (736m) and the distant snow-capped Bla Bheinn (928m). With its close proximity to both the Red Hills and Black Cuillin, Sligachan is still a Mecca for climbers and walkers. Once it was considered to be one of the most famous climbing centres in Europe from where the majority of the Cuillin peaks were first conquered, the most northerly of the Black Cuillin peaks Squrr nan Gillean (964m) being only 5km away. Many climbers now favour Glen Brittle as a base instead. The main Glen Sligachan track leads down to Loch Scavaig and the road to Elgol.

The snow-covered shoulder of Bruach na Frithe (958m) viewed from across Glen Brittle.

In Skye's northeast Trotternish peninsula a spine of high hills and steep cliffs runs parallel to the coast beyond Portree, the island's capital. On the cliff's eastern flank there are numerous signs of vast landslips occurring over thousands of years. Amidst the drama of this wild prehistoric landscape there are many individual geological features to be visited such as the well known rock pinnacle The Old Man of Storr, The Quiraing, castellated crags called The Prison, another pinnacle The Needle and a high flat grassy platform The Table. The photograph looks back from near The Quiraing along these dramatic cliffs above Staffin where hang-gliding is rapidly becoming a new pastime.

Late afternoon light over Trumpan church, Waternish. The remains of the church, once known as Kilconon church, and its surrounding graves lie on a small hill at the extremity of the Waternish peninsula above Ardmore Point. For many this remote, peaceful location with its outstanding views across The Minch to the Western Isles is one of the most beautiful parts of Skye. It is now hard to believe that in 1578 it was the site of a massacre of most of the local inhabitants by the MacDonalds of Uist, the church being set alight during a service. The MacDonalds, however, in retreating too slowly were themselves subsequently killed by the MacLeods from Dunvegan acting in revenge, their bodies being buried under the tumbling of an earthen dyke. The event is still known as the 'Battle of the Spoiling of the Dyke'.

The coral beach at Claigan on the western shore of Loch Dunvegan lies some 8km north of Dunvegan village. It can be reached by a minor road continuing on past the well known castle, seat of the MacLeods, followed by a short track. This beautiful beach, by far the most attractive on Skye, is entirely formed of cast-up coral fragmented to coarse sand and covered by numerous varieties of seashells. The coral is produced by a seaweed called Lithothamnion growing a short distance from the shore.

Rock colours, Elgol.

Black House thatched roofs, Garenin, Lewis. On the west coast of Lewis, north of Carloway, the last remaining street of black houses has been rebuilt to form the Garenin Black House Village Museum. The final residents left in 1973 but many of the buildings have now been restored to give the visitor an indication of life in such structures during the late nineteenth and early twentieth centuries. As explained earlier, many of these primitive cottages would have had a simple hearth in the centre of the floor, the smoke finding its way out through the thatch instead of the use of more conventional chimneys. The walls would have been extremely thick to withstand the prevailing winds and in some cases the crofter's animals would have shared the same shelter.

Colour and abandonment, Lewis. Set amongst the wide ranging hills, moors and lochans a few of the many empty and abandoned traditional croft cottages to be found on Lewis, left either through the death of their former occupants or in favour of more modern, weatherproof and heated homes.

This page and opposite: Peat cutters' huts, the String Road near Stornoway. Peat is still traditionally cut as an everyday fuel throughout much of the Hebrides but in particular on the vast, open, black, peat moors of Lewis where in places mechanical cutting is also used. In early summer, the cut peats are allowed to dry before being transported and stacked at the homes where they will be burnt during the winter months. These flimsy, vulnerable but often colourful huts to be found not just along the String Road but also in other locations such as Cuidhsiadar near Ness would once have been used for the local inhabitants attending the peats during the long summer evenings. However, with the availability of modern transport, many of the buildings are no longer or rarely used. Peat, whilst being a cheap fuel is not particularly efficient. An old Gaelic phrase tells how 'the black peat will warm itself before it warms anybody else'!

Iolaire memorial, Holm Point. On Holm Point to the east of Stornoway harbour stands this simple stone memorial dedicated to the 205 men of Lewis who on New Years Day 1919 were drowned returning home from service at the end of the First World War. Their ship the *Iolaire* was wrecked on rocks known as the Beasts of Holm whilst entering the harbour in full view of their waiting families.

The open sands of Uig. Below the west coast's Gallan Head, Camus Uig and the magnificent sands of Uig between Crowlista and Carnish form one of the best known beaches in the Western Isles. It was here at these flawless sands that a twelfth century Norse chess set was discovered in dunes behind the beach, carved, it is thought, from walrus ivory. Over ninety such figures were collected and are now in the care of the Scottish National Museum in Edinburgh.

Above: Carloway Broch. About 8km north of Callanish the broch at Doune Carloway is one of the finest structures of its type in Scotland. Over 15m in diameter and of similar height, a considerable portion of its double-skinned tapering dry-stone walling still survives. Within these walls the remains of galleries and staircases can readily be seen. As with other brochs, its original use is still uncertain but thought to be for defensive purposes. Its age has been estimated to be at least 2000 years.

Opposite: Callanish Stone Circle. Undoubtedly one of the most significant and important megalithic complexes in Europe, the Callanish I stone circle stands on a low exposed hill above Loch Roag on the west coast of Lewis. It is generally considered to be the second greatest prehistoric structure in Britain after Stonehenge. The circle is thought to be some 4000 years old and until the 1850s when the surrounding peat was removed, the true height of its stones had not been appreciated. The slender great centre stone is 4.5 m high. The cruciform plan of the stones – a circle within a cross using both single and double radiating lines – and their alignment, suggest an astronomical use but this has yet to be proven. Two other smaller circles, Callanish II and III lie in close proximity.

Aignish on the Machair. East of Stornoway, the capital of Lewis and administrative centre of the Western Isles, the densely populated hilly Eye Peninsula stretches to Tiumpan Head overlooking the distant mountains of Sutherland. On the northern shore of the narrow connecting isthmus to the peninsula at Aignish stands the remains of the fourteenth century church of St Columba last used in the 1820s. Nineteen MacLeod chiefs are said to be buried here. In a beautiful longing-for-home song written by Agnes Mure MacKenzie of Stornoway and set to an ancient melody, the church has been immortalised by these moving words:-

> *When day and night are over, and the world is done with me,*
> *Oh carry me west and lay me in Aignish, Aignish by the sea.*
>
> *And never heed me lying amongst the ancient dead,*
> *besides the white sea breakers and sand-drift overhead.*
>
> *The grey gulls wheeling ever, and the wide arch of sky,*
> *On Aignish, Aignish on the machair, and quiet, quiet there to lie.*

Morning light over Loch Roag near Callanish. Loch Roag cuts deeply into the west coast of Lewis with the large island of Great Bernera at its centre linked by the first pre-stressed concrete bridge to be constructed in Europe. Apart from Great Bernera the loch features numerous sheltered bays and a considerable scattering of smaller islands such as Pabay Mor, Vacsay, Vuia Mor, Vuia Beag, Little Bernera, Floday and Keava all now uninhabited but forming one of the most interesting areas on Lewis.

Tràigh Rosamol, Harris. The view looking south along Tràigh Rosamol to the distant 339m Toe Head on the south-west corner of Harris. The deserted shell-sand beach is typical of many to be found on Harris with its beautiful creamy yellow toning enhanced by the intense blue skies and general clarity, a simple indicator of the total lack of industrial pollution. The island of Taransay, now deserted and the setting of a television programme, *Castaway*, some years ago, is on the right of the photograph.

HARRIS AND BERNERAY
Colour, Calm and Cloth

Feather-like sand patterns, Tràigh Rosamol.

Harris lies south of Lewis occupying a relatively small proportion of the same landmass and separated from its much larger adjoining neighbour by a broad barrier of high mountains, the North Harris Hills, and a notable variation of local dialect. Although also sharing a considerable degree of wild, bare, rocky moorland, Harris is blessed with fertile machair along its western shores, and above all its glorious shell-sand beaches. For many a simple vision of the Hebrides spells Harris. With their long, curving, often deeply scalloped bays forming almost the entire west coast, these beaches are not only some of the finest in the British Isles but also in Europe. It is perhaps above all the remarkable contrast between these scenes and the 'lunar' landscape of eastern Harris described in the following pages that provides much of the fascination and interest. On the narrow isthmus created between the sea lochs of East and West Tarbert almost splitting the island into two, lies Tarbert, the small capital of Harris, its timeless quality providing a further attraction.

The wild, rocky but colourful coastal scenery in the vicinity of Hushinish on the far western tip of Harris looking towards the empty island of Scarp on the left and the more distant hills of Aird Mhor and Aird Bheag in the wilderness of south west Lewis. The remains of old homes, some still used as holiday cottages, can be seen above Scarp beach. Even as late as 1940 Scarp had a population approaching 100 but by 1971 all had gone. The island briefly became famous during the 1930s as the location where experiments with rocket-powered mail delivery were carried out but later abandoned due to the unreliability of such technology. Note the intense colouration of the sea over the underlying sand.

Opposite: Tràigh Seilebost beach looking towards the dunes and township of Luskentyre with the stormy North Harris Hills in the far distance. Whilst the much maligned and unpredictable Hebridean weather can be the cause of considerable frustration and hardship, it also has the benefit of allowing such glorious beaches as this to be almost devoid of human activity throughout the year.

Near Toe Head the broad sweeping beach known as Tràigh an Taoibh Thuath floods to a shallow depth at high tide but at low tide takes on an almost desert-like appearance. Under clear blue skies the sand as shown here slowly dries out as the waters retreat. The distant Harris Hills can be seen on the right with the dark shoulder of Toe Head on the left. From the Head on clear days the islands of the St Kilda archipelago some 80km to the west can often be seen.

Bands of colour at Tràigh Scarasta. Scenes such as this are more reminiscent of the islands of the Caribbean or Indian Ocean rather than north-west Scotland.

Sunshine and sparkle on a silver sea and tidal patterns near Luskentyre. As the tidal waters race in or recede across the almost flat sand of Tràigh Losgaintir the colours in the bay and variations in flow patterns change continually every second of the day. Depending on the water depth in the numerous meandering channels the shapes and tones range from the most delicate hues to the most intense of shades aided by the reflected colours of the sky.

Opposite: Colour, texture and aspects of Harris.

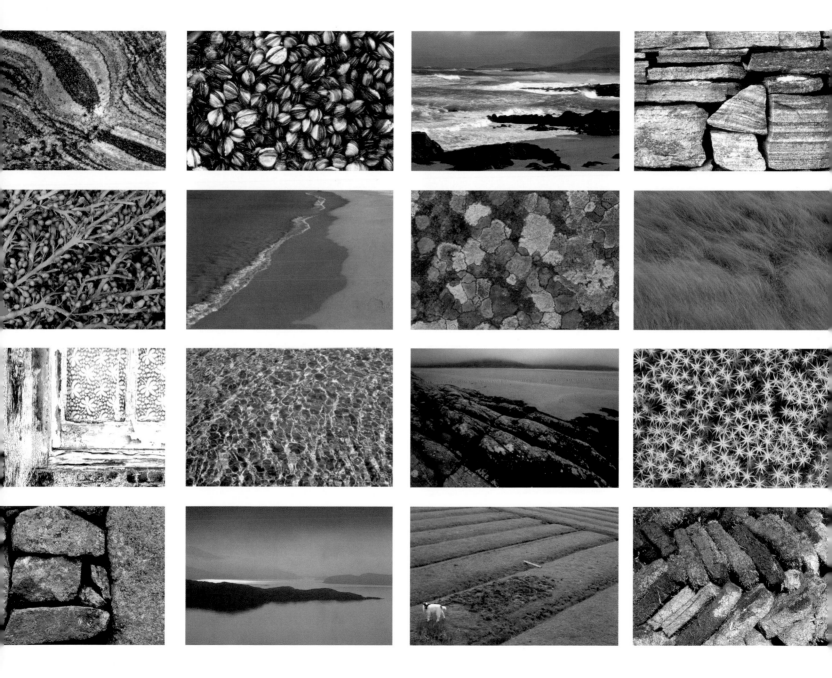

This page and opposite: Harris Tweed. Until the middle of the twentieth century a high proportion of people on Harris wove tweed for their own use. Whole families would be involved from the care of sheep to manufacture of the cloth with recipes of dyes often a closely guarded secret. Any surplus fabric would be sold to help the family economy. Sadly demand for tweed has dropped over the years and at present only a few dedicated weavers still remain on Harris. All over the island the empty weaving sheds can still be seen devoid of their Hattersley single width looms and their history. These photographs show the colourful tweed, inspired by the shades of the Harris landscape, its plants, mosses and lichens, on display at an outlet in Plocrapol on the eastern coast.

A carpet of white sea shells leads to a moody back-drop on a 'soft' morning at Tràigh Seilebost.

Rock design, Port a' Tuath, Hushinish.

School mural, Seilebost. With the slow general population decline of Harris, the number of pupils attending this small, beautifully sited school on the machair at Seilebost is becoming critical. A threat of closure now hangs over the building, its future very much in the balance.

A stormy morning at Tràigh Rosamol with the North Harris Hills beyond and Taransay to the left.

Peat beds near Finsbay.

Opposite: Eastern landscape near Plocrapol looking over Loch Phlocrapoil towards Drinishader. Much of eastern Harris is near naked rock punctuated by tiny lochans and almost utterly devoid of trees and vegetation. With its predominant colours of grey and a sometimes rich peaty brown only relieved by the occasional white painted croft cottage, this desolate terrain is in stark contrast to the lush beaches of western Harris shown earlier. Known as The Bays after the general profile of the coastline, it is this land in which many of the islands' residents still live in a series of small settlements and townships, their ancestors having been forcibly removed from the more fertile west coast during the Highland Clearances. With little natural soil available, coffins once had to be carried back across Harris to the west to be buried. Sustained at one time by only fishing, spinning, weaving and the construction of the cruelly named 'lazybeds' and now finally linked by the narrow, winding and undulating 'Golden Road', the population of this awe-inspiring area of Harris is a remarkable example of human resilience.

This page and opposite: The decay and dereliction of many of the older cheaply constructed croft cottages still acts as a reminder of the hardships of living in such inhospitable landscapes as that of eastern Harris and the extremes of the north western climate.

This page and opposite: Berneray. Although linked by a causeway to North Uist the small island of Berneray is in certain respects a miniature version of Harris. It has a rugged, grassy, undulating and windswept interior but with an extensive coastal flower-filled machair and two glorious white sandy beaches – Port a Chambair to the east and the notable 6km Tràigh Iar along the west. All habitation is also in the east mainly at Borve and Ruisgarry. *Above:* The weather forecasting stone outside the island stores. *Opposite, top left:* The ancient burial ground below Beinn Shieibhe. *Opposite, top right:* Empty black house window. *Opposite, lower left:* A wartime Nissen hut converted to a dwelling. *Opposite, lower right:* Port a Chambair beach with Harris in the distance.

Part of the interior of the church of St Clement at Rodel. The church on the south east tip of Harris above Rodel Harbour is one of the very few surviving ancient buildings in the Hebrides. Built by Alasdair Crotach, the 8th MacLeod at the beginning of the sixteenth century with sandstone transported from Mull, the cruciform church and its rectangular tower are a unique and distinctive feature in the Harris landscape. Within the nave the tomb of Alasdair, richly carved with ornate scenes and figures, is regarded as one of the finest of its type in Scotland.

Opposite: Sunset viewed from Seilebost at high water looking towards Luskentyre and the North Harris Hills.

The Sgurr from Galmisdale. The 393m craggy pitchstone lava monolith of the Sgurr is Eigg's highest point and its most distinguishing geological feature. It not only dominates the island but seen from afar is one of the entire region's most distinctive outlines. Despite its dramatic form, it is easily ascended and the views from its summit were described in 1811 as 'yielding scenes unparalleled in Britain'. The entire 8km x 5km island is a Mecca for geologists due to the multitude of rock forms, high cliffs and evidence of prehistoric volcanic activity still to be found. The building across the flower strewn meadows is Galmisdale House, once the island's inn.

Unusually for a Hebridean island, Eigg features a considerable area of mainly deciduous woodland particularly rising up from the harbour shoreline at Galmisdale. Much was planted around the traditional laird's home 'the Lodge' and intended to act as a windbreak when mature. In places with the later addition of a variety of exotic species, the woodlands have now taken on a semi-tropical nature. During spring the banks, slopes and folds of the woodland floor are often carpetted with bluebell and wild ramson as shown in the photograph.

Laig Bay in a 'soft' grey mood with Rum's peaks covered in low cloud.

Opposite: Another view of the island of Rum from the rocky coastline between Laig Bay and Camus Sgiotaig noted for its 'singing sands'. The rocks can be found in remarkable formations ranging from wide volcanic lava sheets and platforms to mushroom-shaped protrusions, dramatic cliff overhangs, narrow passageways, natural arches, water-filled pots and fissures, rounded concretions and a network of often deep basaltic dykes angling their way to Rum. In places waterfalls can be heard and burns tumble to the sea in vast natural rock gardens.

Aspects of Eigg. The photograph (top left) shows the wind-powered element of the island's new award-winning electrification system also incorporating solar and hydro-created energy.

Top left: The nineteenth century Church of Scotland church, its surrounding trees shrouded in mist.

Bottom right: The one remaining cottage left after the two crofting townships of Upper and Lower Grulin were cleared in 1853. Used after as a shepherd's bothy it is now a holiday home backed by the steep flanks of the Sgurr.

The living room complete with cooker and the fireplace added in the early years of the twentieth century.

The main bedroom.

This page and opposite: Tigh Iain Dhonnachaidh, Eigg's Museum of Crofting Life. This new museum, opened in 2009, features one of the very last undeveloped cottages on the island and as such has become a veritable time capsule. It offers a unique glimpse of the life of its former inhabitants, the Campbell family – crofters of Cleadale from the 1900s to the 1990s. The family moved in when the building was still a thatched black house, improving the facilities and crucially adding chimneys, gable ends, a new roof and interior partitions. The abundance of everyday objects and original furnishings left in the house make it a superb location for the study of Eigg's social history. Also on display are archive photographs and documents relating to the family.

Late evening light looking over Eigg's eastern fields towards the Sound of Arisaig, the distant hills of Moidart and Knoydart and the town of Mallaig.

Sunset behind Rum viewed from Laig Bay. Whilst being heavily reliant on a network of ferries to sustain their liveli-hood and provide a lifeline to the outside world, the Small Isles allow no visitors' cars to be taken to the islands – just foot passengers only. For many who come here in these days of instant technology and fast global travel this is possi-bly the greatest attraction of all. The Hebrides are acknowledged as an utterly special environment that has so far escaped the ravages and worst excesses of twenty-first century living. These four small islands with Eigg in particular, offer something even more unique – a certain sense of inner peace and tranquility and to a degree a richness and quality of life that has all but disappeared from nearly all our shores and lives. We can all learn from this. Long may it continue.

> *"Egge ..... gude mayne land, with ane paroch kirk in it, with mony solenne geis; very gude*
> *for store, namelie for scheip, with one heavin for heiland Galayis."*

> Dean Monro, *A description of the Western Isles of Scotland called Hybrides, 1549.*

ACKNOWLEDGEMENTS

Once again inspiration for these photographs has come from many visits to Western Scotland and the Hebrides in the course of which I have met numerous islanders and photographers. To all of them I owe a certain debt, not only for their kindness, patience and encouragement but also for the revelation of a lifestyle where many traditional values are still appreciated, for the discovery of a landscape and environment that can only be described as unique and the realisation that 'time' is not quite so important as our modern culture leads us to believe. To all of you my grateful thanks but especially to:

Ken and Polly Bryan; Fiona Doyle; Camille Dressler; Ursula Goundry; Margaret Kirk; Pat MacNab; Catherine Morrison; Pat and Cathy Myhill; Jon and Linda Pear.

As always particular thanks go to Joy once more for her infinite patience, support and hard work in typing the manuscript and finally, yet again, to Steven Pugsley and his enthusiastic colleagues at Halsgrove for all their faith and assistance.

REFERENCE SOURCES

There are numerous books, booklets, papers, leaflets and guides about Western Scotland and the Hebridean islands.
It is virtually impossible to mention them all but the following have been invaluable as reference sources:

Banks, N *Six Inner Hebrides* David and Charles, 1977
Berneray Community Association *Island of Berneray*, 1990
Campbell, A *Island of Eigg – a short guide*, 1995
Cooper, D *Skye* Routledge and Kegan Paul, 1970
Cornish, J *Scotland's Coast* Aurum, 2005
Craig, D and Paterson, D *The Glens of Silence* Birlinn, 2004
Dressler, C *Eigg, the story of an Island* Birlinn, 2007
Haswell Smith, H *The Scottish Islands* Canongate, 1996
Lawson, B *Harris in History and Legend* John Donald, 2002
MacDonald, A and P *The Highlands and Islands of Scotland* Weidenfeld and Nicholson, 1991
MacEwen, L *The Island of Muck* 1998
McGowan, I *Hebridean Images* Creative Monochrome, 1993
McGowan, I *Portrait of the Hebrides* Halsgrove, 2008
Milsom, H *Mood and Colour* Hugh Milsom Photography, 2007
Murray, W *The West Highlands of Scotland* Collins, 1973

Murray, W *The Hebrides* Heinemann, 1969
Nicholson, A *Sea Room* Harper Collins, 2001
Paterson, D *The Cape Wrath Trail* Peak Publishing, 1996
Patterson, D *A long walk on the Isle of Skye* Peak Publishing, 1999
Patterson, D *A Scottish Journey* Wildcountry Press, 2003
Rixon, D *The Small Isles* Birlinn, 2001
Urquhart, J and Ellington, E *Eigg* Canongate, 1987
Wade Martin, S *Eigg and Island Landscape* Countryside Publishing, 1987
Wright, A and Banning, T *Arran* 2006
Wylie, G *The Hebrides* Collins, 1978
Wylie, G *Patterns of the Hebrides* A Zwemmer, 1981
Wylie, G *Hebridean Light* Birlinn, 2003
Pearce, A and Watkins, D *Land of Hearts Desire – Songs of the Hebrides* Meridian Records, 1975